'Tis The Night Before Jesus

by Robert Mueller

'TIS THE NIGHT BEFORE JESUS

9157 / ISBN 1-55673-358-5

PRINTED IN U.S.A.

'Tis The Night Before Jesus

By Robert Mueller

C.S.S. Publishing Company, Inc.
Lima, Ohio

Order Of Service

'tis the night before jesus

Processional Song by the Congregation: "O Come, All Ye Children"

Call to Worship:

Leader: We meet here in the name of God, who is Father, Son and Holy Spirit.

People: These words are first spoken over us in our baptism, in which we die with Christ and are raised with him to a new life with God.

Leader: We meet here to celebrate and to reflect upon the birth of Jesus at Bethlehem.

People: Help us to see, dear Lord, that we cannot create or program your gifts — we can only receive them!

Leader: Help us to see, dear Lord, that for those involved in the birth of Jesus, faith is not easy.

All: Give us your Holy Spirit, dear Lord, that we will believe your Word, and live a special, different life according to it. Amen.

Song by the Congregation and Children: "Oh, How Joyfully, Oh, How Merrily"

Speech Choir

Song by Children: "In A Little Stable"

Speech Choir

Song by Children: "Hark! The Herald Angels Sing"

Speech Choir

Mary Tells About the Night Before Jesus

Song by Children: "Away In A Manger"

Speech Choir

Song by the Congregation: "Let All Together Praise Our God"

Speech Choir and the Congregation:

Christ is on earth, the old is like new,
    Now people can see what God can do.
Where children hurt and old people whistle,
    Where there are fir trees and dry prickly thistle.
Tis the night before Jesus from ground to the sky,
    And Jesus, our brother, will surely come by!
So we know and you know that heaven is in sight,
    Good morning to all, and to all a good night!

Song by Children: "Deck The Halls To Greet The Savior"

A Final Blessing:

> Leader: In the name of God the Father,
>
> **People: Who is our creator, owner and protector;**
>
> Leader: In the name of God the Son,
>
> **People: Who brings us salvation, forgiveness and health;**
>
> Leader: In the name of God the Holy Spirit,
>
> **People: Who brings all of God's gifts to and through people just like us! Amen.**

Recessional Song by the Congregation and Children: "Joy To The World!"

A Christmas Service For The
Congregation And Its Children

'tis the night before jesus

Processional Song by the Congregation: "O Come, All Ye
Children"
*(As the children enter, have them bring an item of food,
clothing or toy for needy families and their children,
and place these gifts in a box in an appropriate
place.)*

Call to Worship:

Leader: We meet here in the name of God, who is Father,
Son and Holy Spirit.

**People: These words are first spoken over us in our bap-
tism, in which we die with Christ and are raised with
him to a new life with God.**

Leader: We meet here to celebrate and to reflect upon the birth of Jesus at Bethlehem.

People: Help us to see, dear Lord, that we cannot create or program your gifts — we can only receive them!

Leader: Help us to see, dear Lord, that for those involved in the birth of Jesus, faith is not easy.

All: Give us your Holy Spirit, dear Lord, that we will believe your Word, and live a special, different life according to it. Amen — that's the way it is and will be!

Song by the Congregation and Children: "Oh, How Joyfully, Oh, How Merrily"

Speech Choir (all):

'Tis the night before Jesus when all through the earth,
Every creature is stirring for a new baby's birth.
The people are looking straight up and then down,
To the left and the right in country and town.
Some faces are watching far out in the sky,
Hoping God's Son will soon be coming by.

Song by Children: "In A Little Stable"

Speech Choir (all):

In Bethlehem children are snug in their beds,
With dreams of olives and figs in their heads.
Sheep are ba-a-ahing their last sleepy bleat,
And the shepherds are tired, weary and beat.

Speech Choir (boys):

When up in the air there arises such a clatter,
The shepherds see angels and ask, "What's the matter?"
They jump to their feet and stand straight and tall,
And see thousands of angels, and hear heaven's call.

10

Song by Children: "Hark! The Herald Angels Sing"

Speech Choir (girls):

> It sounds like glory, looks bright as can be,
> It's hard to believe — it's hard to see.
> When what to their wondering eyes does appear,
> But glory around them so loud and so near.
> It happens so sudden, it happens so quick.
> Is it real? Is it true? Or is it a trick?

Speech Choir (all):

> More rapid than eagles the shepherds they run,
> Find Mary and Joseph, and their newborn son.
> "He's Yahweh's Servant, David's Son,
> Emmanuel, Prince of Peace, all and each one!"
> They fall to their knees way down on the ground,
> How good to receive him — the one they have found.
> The shepherds see Jesus, for joy they do cry.
> For Jesus the Savior has surely come by.
> So straight up the hillsides their running feet fly.
> "Angels appear to people like us," they wonder why.

Mary Tells About the Night Before Jesus:

My name is Mary, of Nazareth in Galilee. My little town isn't even mentioned in our holy writings. In Judea, it's a common joke that nothing good can come out of Nazareth! Because there are some Assyrians way back in our family tree, Judean folks, when they see us coming, sometimes they cross over to the other side of the street.

My grandfather once served as a priest in Jerusalem. But I grew up as an orphan. My parents both died soon after I was born. I was raised by some kind-hearted neighbors here in Nazareth. They keep telling me that I'm from the royal family of King David, from whose line the Messiah is to come. But as an orphan and a cleaning woman, I don't feel very special.

11

There are some women in David's family tree that must feel like I do. There's Tamar, the daughter-in-law of our ancestor, Judah. To get a son, because her husband dies, she dresses up like a prostitute, and has relations with Judah.

Then there's Rahab, of Jericho. She saves the life of the 12 men that Moses sends to spy out the promised land. Ruth, a direct ancestor of David, isn't Jewish, either. Her first husband dies, and she comes with her mother-in-law to our strange land. But these are the women that the Almighty uses at critical times in our history. Since we haven't seen a prophet in almost 400 years, I wonder if the Messiah will come in my lifetime.

I'm at home one day when I get the feeling that someone is watching me. When I look out the lattice window into the courtyard, I see bright rays of light out there. I unbolt the door and peek out. Then a voice says to me, "Greetings, you who are greatly blessed. The Lord is with you." My heart is pounding like a blacksmith's hammer when the voice says, "Stop being afraid, Mary. God has chosen to bless you."

"There's that word "blessed" again! I don't feel very happy, fortunate or complete. I'm an orphan, a mere cleaning woman — promised in marriage to a man much older than I am," I'm saying to myself. The voice breaks into my daydreams and says that I'm going to conceive a son, and that I should name him Jesus, that the Almighty will give him the throne of his ancestor David, that he will be our king forever!

The voice says that the Spirit of the Almighty will brood over me like it did in creation, that the one to be born from me will be called the Son of God. Then I remember that my cousin, Elizabeth, in her old age is six months pregnant. Her husband, Zacharias, says an angel tells him their son will be another Elijah. The voice must be reading my mind because it says, "There is nothing that God will not be able to do." I hear myself say, "I belong to Yahweh. Let it happen just as you say!" As suddenly as it appears, the bright light is gone.

For a long time, I'm confused about what happened, and I'm afraid to tell any of this to Joseph. Because I'm scared, I stay away from Joseph. From what the neighbors say, he doesn't seem to want to talk to me, either.

Finally, as the Sabbath begins one evening, there is a timid knock on my door. It's Joseph! I look to see if he has a letter of divorce in his hand. No . . . his hands are shaking, but they're empty! I'm shaking, too, as Joseph says, "Mary . . . we have to talk." I'm both scared and strangely at peace.

I hear Joseph say, "The Blessed One tells me . . ." There's a long pause, and Joseph's forehead is wet. "In a dream," Joseph starts over, "the Lord's angel says you have conceived a son by the Holy Spirit, and that he shall be called 'Jesus,' for he will save his people from their sins."

In my joy, I hug Joseph, "That's what the Blessed One tells me, too! But I've been afraid to say anything to you!" Joseph says he's been scared, too. He says he's afraid I'll think he's become like one of those strange people in the Dead Sea community!

"It's not that God can't do any of this," we tell each other. "What's amazing is that the Anointed One will be born of an orphan, a cleaning woman from Nazareth, who will marry a carpenter whose specialty is making ox yokes!"

Joseph and I are married. But before we can really get to know each other, we hear that the Caesar in Rome has ordered a census. Augustus wants people counted so he can see if his tax agents are collecting too much, or not enough! Since there's so much divorce in the Empire, he also wants to see how his marriage program is working.

Joseph says it's just as well, that he's ready to move someplace else, anyway. And we do have relatives in Bethlehem. As far along as I am with the baby, I dread the three-day trip. But I know the Messiah is supposed to be born in David's home town. Joseph and I laugh that it takes a Caesar to get that done!

Ever since King David makes Jerusalem his capital, everybody calls it "the city of David." But the Messiah won't be born in the capital city. As the prophet Micah says, he'll be born in tiny Bethlehem, where the teen-age David once took care of sheep! That's how the Blessed One gives gifts: where you'd least expect it!

As we make the long trip to Bethlehem, I pet our faithful little donkey, and I keep humming to myself, "My soul magnifies the Lord, and my spirit delights in God, who vindicates me! I'm only an orphaned cleaning woman, but God looks kindly upon me. People through all generations will call me blessed — because Yahweh does great things for me!"

Song by Children: "Mary's Little Boy Child"

Speech Choir (girls):

> Far away, wise men stand on some roof,
>> Searching the skies for religious proof.
> Night after night they hunt with care,
>> For a sign of God's love in some stars out there.

Speech Choir (boys):

> One wise man with gold has a little round tummy,
>> The frankincense wise man smells yummy yum
>> yummy.
> The gift of rare myrrh is packed in a can,
>> For Jesus will need it when he's a man!

Speech Choir (boys):

> They are soon filled with questions from head to toe,
>> "Where's the newborn king? We truly must know!"
> They travel so long and journey so far,
>> They follow their hearts — guided by the star.

Speech Choir (all):

Herod and the Bible experts make them grim for a while,
  Then slowly each face returns to a smile.
They see God give his Son quietly in birth,
  They take up God's gift, putting theirs on the earth.
There's no more to do, there's no more to say,
  This is God's world and this is God's day.
As the baby blinks while turning his head,
  The wise men know they have nothing to dread.
They speak not a word as they head back home,
  They thank God that Jesus the Savior is come!

Song by the Congregation: "Let All Together Praise Our God"

Speech Choir and Congregation:

Christ is on earth, the old is like new,
  Now people can see what God can do.
Where children hurt and old people whistle,
  Where there are fir trees and dry prickly thistle.
Tis the night before Jesus from ground to the sky,
  And Jesus, our brother, will surely come by!
So we know and you know that heaven is in sight,
  Good morning to all, and to all a good night!

Song by Children: "Deck The Halls To Greet The Savior"

A Final Blessing:

Leader: In the name of God the Father,

People: Who is our creator, owner and protector;

Leader: In the name of God the Son,

People: Who brings us salvation, forgiveness and health;

15

Leader: In the name of God the Holy Spirit,

People: Who brings all of God's gifts to and through people just like us! Amen — that's how it is and will be!

Recessional Song by Congregation and Children: "Joy To The World!"

Printed below are the words of the song, "Deck The Halls To Greet The Savior":

Deck the halls to greet the Savior!
    Come and praise the Lord! Alleluia!
Celebrate his gracious favor!
    Come and praise the Lord! Alleluia!
For the joyous gospel story
    Praise the Lord! Praise him! Alleluia!
Till he comes again in glory
    Come and praise the Lord! Alleluia!

(The text for the song "Deck The Halls To Greet The Savior" is from "Here He Comes," by Arden W. Mead, Creative Communications for the Parish, St. Louis, MO, copyright 1982. Used by permission. The song is sung to the melody of "Deck the Halls.")

Alternative songs to be used with 'Tis the Night Before Jesus:

"Thy Little Ones, Dear Lord, Are We"
(Use music of "From Heaven Above")

"I Wonder As I Wander"

"There Was No Room for Mary there"
(A Christmas carol from Mexico)

"As Each Happy Christmas"

"What Star Is This, Which Beams So Bright?"

"Mary Had a Baby"

O Lord, We Welcome Thee"

"What Child Is This?"

"Jesus, Our Brother, Kind and Good"

"Come, Jesus, Holy Child, to Me"

"When Christmas Morn is Dawning"
(From "Service Book and Hymnal")

"This Is Our Way to Remember"
(By Carolyn Hardin Englehardt; music by F. Gruber; arranged by P. Faber)